TREES, BIRDS, AND FIRE

TREES, BIRDS, AND FIRE

How Musicians and Artists Can Leverage Web 3.0 to Build Fan Engagement

Jamil Hasan

TREES, BIRDS, AND FIRE

Table of Contents

Introducing the Crypto Hipster's Chronicles   5

Chapter 1: Why Artists Should Create Their Own Platforms for Fan Engagement   9

Chapter 2: How Artists and Scientists Are Paving the Path for NFTs in Film and Painting   27

Chapter 3: The Duality of Life as Half Man, Half Cyborg   49

Chapter 4: The Challenges of Building a Metaverse Entertainment Platform   81

Appendix A: About the Author   107

Appendix B: Crypto Hipster Podcasts   113

Appendix C: Crypto Hipster's Chronicles   143

TREES, BIRDS, AND FIRE

Introducing the Crypto Hipster's Chronicles

During my five plus years in the cryptocurrency, digital asset, and blockchain industry, I have accomplished a variety of things in the space, including authoring this book, my seventh book, with many more to come, and hosting over 190 podcasts. My Crypto Hipster Podcasts (anchor.fm/crypto-hipster-podcast) differ from post other cryptocurrency podcasts. While the top venture capital studios focused on price and market action of Bitcoin, alternative coins, NFTs and metaverses, I focused on something else:

The long-term societal and personal benefits of blockchain technology use cases, globally.

I then compiled three to five individual podcasts at a time to create Crypto Hipster's Chronicles. These compilations are more than just a catchy compilation. They all center around a common

TREES, BIRDS, AND FIRE

theme, a theme based on "human" issues. These human issues include societal, mindset, social skills, and personal growth and development.

I have titled the tenth compilation for Crypto Hipster's Chronicles, Episode 10, "Leveraging Web 3.0 to Build Fan Engagement", and that episode I have now converted into this book.

Contrary to the wishes of existing Big Tech incumbents, the future of NFTs and the metaverse are based on decentralization and on correcting the global mistakes we made during the evolution of the Web 2.0 internet. Musicians and artists are now able to take control of their creations and build intimate fan engagement. Concerts are being held in the Metaverse with greater attendance than physical venues. Artists now have unprecedented global reach and can collaborate easily with scientists and other experts. And content creators from all spectrums of the art world can build a loyal following where they control and own the information necessary to directly engage closely with their fans.

This twelfth book in the Crypto Hipster series, entitled **Trees, Birds, and Fire** focuses on four Crypto Hipster podcasts. Sam Feldt, world famous disc jockey, music producer, and founder of Fangage, founder of TKS, shares why musicians should create their own platform for fan engagement. Christian Hook, painter and film producer shares how artists and scientists, collaboratively are paving the path for NFTs in film and painting. He discusses his experiences with his latest documentary *Painting the Invisible*. Musician Orrin tells us what it is like to be half man and half cyborg and his inner struggles of duality with the creation of his album MUTANTS. And Colin Fitzpatrick, Chief Executive Officer of Animal Concerts, tells all about the challenges of building a global concert platform in the metaverse.

TREES, BIRDS, AND FIRE

My hope is that you find this book both educational and useful in your crypto and life journey.

Disclaimer: Most casual conversations in my podcasts were in the passive voice. To author this book and make it enjoyable, I have translated the content to the active voice as much as possible while maintaining the intent of my guests' answers and responses. I have provided links to all the original conversations at the beginning of each chapter. I welcome you to listen to the podcasts besides reading this book.

Chapter 1— Why Artists Should Create Their Own Platforms for Fan Engagement

DJ, producer, entrepreneur, and sustainability pioneer **Sam Feldt** has established himself as one of the most sought-after electronic artists of recent times. Building his career around distinctly feel-good sound, Sam already has a double album and a multitude of top-selling releases under his belt. The platinum-selling DJ and producer has proven himself to be an entrepreneur at heart, with his own platform Fangage - meant for artists to connect with their fans better - and the launch of his own record label Heartfeldt Records in 2020.

On top of this, with his project Heartfeldt Foundation, Sam is passionately working towards a more social and sustainable dance music industry. With this foundation, he promotes a sustainable lifestyle according to the Do-Give-Inspire and Empower model and aims to combine the reach of a

TREES, BIRDS, AND FIRE

lot of different influencers to create awareness around sustainability issues. The mission of the foundation is a common thread for the entire Heartfeldt business chain: Heartfeldt Records, Heartfeldt Radio and Heartfeldt Events. Both in music and life, Sam has his sights set firmly on the future.

Heartfeldt Foundation

In his entrepreneurship, Sam is always looking for ways to help others and protect our planet. This same philosophy will apply to Sam's extracurricular endeavor to mitigate the climate impact of his DJ activities as much as possible. He is known as a DJ and he flies all over the world and thus has a large carbon footprint. For this reason, his flight behavior is measured, visitors to Heartfeldt events are asked about their way of transport to his shows and 1% of the stream earnings of Heartfeldt Records releases go to Heartfeldt Foundation. "The whole idea is to maximize the impact of what I'm doing," Sam elaborates. "The transition to a circular economy is something that we are all part of and I think companies and people who are trying to do their best for the environment should get attention and support." As an ambassador of Plastic Promise, Plastic Soup Foundation and partner of Blondish Bye Bye Plastic, many positive adjustments are already made within the events sector. Sam Feldt believes sustainability is needed in all areas of our consumption. He is therefore open to collaborating with all interested parties to investigate how life, from everyday consumption of food and drinks to flying and performing music, can be made sustainable.

Original Interview Date: November 13, 2021
Original Interview Link: https://spotifyanchor-web.app.link/e/epqs8eTUsvb

CRYPTO HIPSTER: Hello, everybody. Welcome to the Crypto Hipsters Podcast where I interview founders and co-founders, entrepreneurs and

TREES, BIRDS, AND FIRE

artists, executives, and stay at home hipsters in crypto and blockchain around the world. I have an amazing podcast for you today. Let us get to it.

Today, courtesy of Web Summit, my amazing guest is Sam Feldt. He is a famous DJ, and the founder of Fangage. Sam, welcome.

Sam: Thank you. Thanks for having me at the show. Appreciate it.

CRYPTO HIPSTER: You're welcome. You're welcome. You're welcome. I was doing backflips when I found out I was going to be interviewing you. So, that was great. So, let us kick things off. What is your background? And is it a logical background for what you are doing now?

Sam: I have been an entrepreneur since I was 13 years old. I had to drag my dad to the Chamber of Commerce to get registered because, of course, I was a minor. I have launched a lot of digital

TREES, BIRDS, AND FIRE

businesses, for example, Social Media Services, dating sites, but also web shops and ecommerce. Outside of that, I have always been a disc jockey and a music producer since I was about 11 years old. Those two collided and I am now the founder of Fangage, which is a startup that gives creators their own platforms. We even have animals and worldwide touring artists. It makes sense.

CRYPTO HIPSTER: For those who do not know your music, could you walk us through a bit of your songs and the story behind them?

Sam: I invite you to go to Sam Feldt on Spotify and just clicked the top three songs. I am sure you know one of them at least. I launched my musical career when I was 11 years old. But it first became successful with Spinnin Records when I was about 21 years old. My first major hit was *Show Me Love*, a remake of the 1993 classic by Robin S. That song peaked at number two in the UK charts. That was a good start. I toured the world after that release and then had a hit song called *Post Malone*, two years ago. Fourteen million listeners on Spotify every month. Definitely. music that you have heard before, on the radio or on your favorite digital signal processor.

CRYPTO HIPSTER: Let us talk about Fangage. What is it all about? How does it work?

Sam: What I discovered as an artist back in 2016 was that I was getting increased followers on social media but reaching less of them. Because of the algorithms, I had to pay Mark Zuckerberg over in Silicon Valley to contact and reach my fan base. Even though they went to my page, they clicked the button; I want to follow Sam Feldt; I like Sam Feldt; I could not contact them to promote my music or let them know about my shows.

I realized I needed to take control of my audience and my fan base. And the only way to do that is if you own fan data, because that really makes you

TREES, BIRDS, AND FIRE

independent of any platform. You simply always have the data to rely on. I started Fangage as a solution to that. We are saying any creator can launch their own fan platform. Fans can sign up to that platform to unlock exclusive content. And in exchange, the creator gets access to their data. We have monetization features that are a little like Patreon and Only Fans, where you can sell subscriptions and content to your fans. And the good thing is that it all runs on your domain and your brand, like Shopify for creators. Instead of sending their fans from one third-party platform to another, you are sending them to your own website, which runs on Fangage, which is completely branded and white labeled. So that is the core idea of getting past the Facebook algorithms.

CRYPTO HIPSTER: What about the Google algorithms?

Sam: For creators, Google is not a big discovery platform. If you Google a creator like Sam Feldt, you usually already know who it is. The networks we target are mostly Instagram, TikTok, and Snap, because those are discovery platforms that allow creators like me to be discovered. We are not saying stop using social media or social media is bad. But use it in a way such that it is a discovery platform and as a traffic source, where the social network is not the destination for your fans. The ultimate destination should always be a platform that is under your control. Just look at what happened to Myspace. Even look at Donald Trump on social media. People are getting banned and their platforms are disappearing. If you do not secure your audience on a platform that is your own, you will be very vulnerable to those types of risks.

CRYPTO HIPSTER: How can content creators take their data back? How do you see it playing out for Web 3.0?

Sam: Web 3.0 is super interesting, like a new way to not only take back control over that data but also own a piece of the pie to which you are contributing. That is something that we are integrating, tokenized access to content and creator tokens that live on the creator platforms. These are all things that we are integrating, but simply, it is all about taking your followers from the algorithm that they are locked into and funneling them to a platform where you control the rules, and you decide for yourself how you interact with your fans. So that they can be engaged. It can also be as simple as an email list. It can also be as simple as your own website. But make sure that your fans live on a platform that is yours, and not only on a platform that is borrowed, because that is obviously not very sustainable.

CRYPTO HIPSTER: I have been in crypto for in blockchain for a few years and noticed many people seem to be anti-technology. How can they adopt a better tech mindset?

TREES, BIRDS, AND FIRE

Sam: Technology is beautiful if you use it the right way. I am a big nerd myself. I am a music producer, which by itself means that I am pro technology. All my music is made electronically. I just think that interests should be aligned. And my interests are not aligned with Facebook. When I get my fans to like my page on Facebook, what I am truthfully saying to them is, hey, come join this platform that sells your data to the highest bidder, does not care about our relationships, and just wants to monetize from the intimate relationship that we have. If we can use tech for the right purposes, and to align our interests instead, it is beautiful. With Fangage, we cut out the middleman; we give that power back where it belongs... to the creator and to their fans. We make that relationship so that third party platforms do not have access to fan data. The only person who has access to your data is the creator that you signed up for. That makes it transparent and very permission based. And it is a great alternative to social media.

TREES, BIRDS, AND FIRE

CRYPTO HIPSTER: You've seen this launch of Meta. How are we going to be affected by Meta? And how can my friends move forward into this new Metaverse society?

Sam: It really depends on how Facebook will roll out their vision and version of the metaverse. How they see it is as some sort of virtual reality world where we interact with each other. But the metaverse will not be centralized. I do not know if the version of the metaverse from Facebook is going to be what ends up being the metaverse. It is extremely hard to predict because the only thing I have seen so far is a video and a vision, which does not align well with how Web 3.0 fuses to the metaverse that inherently has an ownership component where creators and fans owns a piece of the pie to which they are contributing. I cannot answer that question, because I do not know what Facebook is going to do in the future. Or if Facebook's way is the right way forward.

TREES, BIRDS, AND FIRE

CRYPTO HIPSTER: There are a lot of positive thoughts and negative thoughts about NFTs, especially for musicians, for performers, and for artists. How do you see the NFT space playing out for musicians? And how can that benefit content creators?

Sam: What's great is that you can tokenize and sell anything that has demand. I am an investor of a startup called Sound XYZ, they are doing NFTs, and are a tokenized SoundCloud. When we integrate tokenized access into Fangage, you could buy a Sam Feldt NFT, which is a piece of splendid music combined with an outstanding visual from my art director. Not only would you get that, but you would also get access to a lot of exclusive content and experiences on my Fangage platform, because Fangage sees that you are a holder of my NFT through meta wallets connection. That really opens a whole new world to reward investors in creators. And these are all about investing in someone you love who makes great content, music, or artwork,

TREES, BIRDS, AND FIRE

and then also reaping the benefits from it when that creator becomes more successful. NFTs are a wonderful way to align interests between fans, supporters, and creators.

CRYPTO HIPSTER: Great, and how do you see the opportunities with Web 3.0 as a game-changer? In the traditional world, we are told to be a lawyer, a doctor, or an accountant or whatever. Do not be a performer. But you are a successful performer. How do you see that Web 3.0 space helping common artists and performers?

Sam: Web 3.0 removes the gatekeeper. There is no art gallery needed any more to highlight and sell your art. Coinbase is launching NFTs and if you make great art, and there is a market for it, then you do not need that middleman anymore to profit from it. You can sustain a career as a creator or as an artist. It helps take down the walls that are around certain industries. And it allows for many more direct monetization possibilities for smaller

TREES, BIRDS, AND FIRE

artists. Right now, you must make millions of streams of your song on Spotify to earn a living. But you only need one thousand fans buying your NFT to make a living. It will be much easier for smaller creators and artists to get to do this full time. That will boost creativity and be a remarkable thing for especially smaller artists.

CRYPTO HIPSTER: How do you see platforms like Fangage and other platforms like yours improving loyalty?

Sam: They do completely because they aligned the interest. If you are a fan of my music, and you sign up to Fangage, and you unlock more content experiences by giving me more information about yourself, that allows me to send you a text message when I am playing a show wherever you are based and that dramatically increases loyalty. I can make sure that I reach you so you will not feel left out. Whenever I have updated content, you are always going to be up to date, no matter what the algorithm does. You will not miss a show or my recent music. That by itself already increases loyalty because you are in the loop. Stack that, together with your interest in my success by holding an NFT that is growing in value, you are going to be more loyal. You are invested. You have ownership interest with a specific creator as well... skin in the game. It will help to increase not only fan engagement but also loyalty.

CRYPTO HIPSTER: One thing I noticed in crypto is the successful projects are the ones where the entrepreneur perseveres when they are backed against the wall when a normal person would quit. I am sure that quitting is rampant in the art, acting, and music industry. What words of encouragement would you offer to new aspiring artists to stay there no matter what? What can they learn from you?

Sam: I have had that moment many times. I have always said to myself, yes, I am going to give myself another year. And if that does not pan out, I must

TREES, BIRDS, AND FIRE

find myself a normal job. But luckily, after a few of these deadlines, I got some traction; I got signed. But that took me 10 years.

I started disc jockeying when I was 11 years old, producing shortly after, and then only got signed to a big label when I was 21 years old. Ten years of trying, failing, and getting back up again. You never know how close you are. And the same counts for starting a startup, for example. It is all about just keeping on, going on, and trying again until you find that sweet spot or that traction that you are looking for. What I would suggest is to stick to it. Make music or artwork that you love, because if you make what you like, there is going to be an audience for it. Just do not imitate because that has already been done before. That is my word of advice.

CRYPTO HIPSTER: My favorite Sam Feldt song is *Stronger*, sung by Kesha. If you could pick any three of your favorite songs, what would they be? And why?

TREES, BIRDS, AND FIRE

Sam: It is hard to say. I have heard those songs too many times. Nostalgically, *Show Me Love* would have to be on that list, because that is what kickstarted it for me and made it possible to roll into future songs as well. Another is a more obscure remix that I have done called *On Trees & Birds & Fire*. Just look it up on YouTube. No other people know it. But that is musically, one of my favorites. And then I think the final one would be *Post Malone*.

CRYPTO HIPSTER: My wife and my kids love *Post Malone*. And they asked me to tell you they love your work.

Sam: Well, say hi and thank you.

CRYPTO HIPSTER: Thank you very much for your time today. How can people find out more information about you, about Fangage, and about your work? How can they engage with you?

TREES, BIRDS, AND FIRE

Sam: Yes, well, my favorite platform is artstyle.me. If you want to check out all my content, you can go over there. Fangage.com is where you can start your own fan platform if you are a creator. It is completely free. So do that. If you want to take more control over your audience and your fan base, just dive in. You will be able to find me.

TREES, BIRDS, AND FIRE

Chapter 2— How Artists and Scientists Are Paving the Path for NFTs in Film and Painting

Christian Hook enlisted the help of several scientists specializing in theoretical physics, physiology, sensory perception and more. Together they explored and broke down a series of ideas and discovered that artists and scientists have more in common than they thought. With their collaboration, Christian embarked on his greatest challenge yet - Painting the Invisible. You can watch some clips from the fascinating film in our interactive catalogue, which includes an online narrated tour of the complete exhibition, behind-the-scenes photography, and, of course, the complete collection of original and limited-edition artwork.

https://www.clarendonfineart.com/news/christian-hook-painting-the-invisible/

TREES, BIRDS, AND FIRE

Bio: https://www.nationalgalleries.org/art-and-artists/artists/christian-hook

The Painting the Invisible video link here: https://www.sky.com/watch/title/programme/3ecdd7d0-7a37-48dc-84c8-058e939355df

The Painting the Invisible artwork images that are only exhibited at Clarendon Fine Art Dover Street: https://we.tl/t-FIMtmozPqp

Original Interview Date: October 30, 2021
Original Interview Link: https://spotifyanchor-web.app.link/e/p0jBJ3SVsvb

CRYPTO HIPSTER: Welcome to the Crypto Hipster Podcast where I interview founders and co-founders, entrepreneurs and artists, executives, and stay at home hipsters in crypto and blockchain around the world. I have an amazing podcast for you today. I have a film producer, a filmmaker. His name is Christian Hook. Christian, welcome to the show today.

Christian: Thank you for having me.

CRYPTO HIPSTER: You're welcome. So, kicking things off, what is your background? And is it a logical background for what you do now?

Christian: Well, I do not think it is logical. I studied illustration at Middlesex University. It was a technical illustration. And then I went into music and recorded a few albums with a local band in Gibraltar, and we had some success in Spain. I was a lecturer at the Royal at the Royal College of Art. I have changed jobs many times and done many things. But I think that when I started doing fine art, I started exhibiting and doing more creative things; I met this artist in Barcelona who inspired me. I started doing completely abstract work. I have ended up doing everything in the fine art world. I have done some documentaries for Sky TV. After living with celebrities, I do a portrait of them. And a lot of the portraits ended up in the national galleries in the UK, and in Seoul. That was really something I did not expect. From then on, I have just gone from bigger things to bigger things. Now I am in a beautiful place. It has been an amazing journey.

CRYPTO HIPSTER: Let us discuss your recent film, *Painting the Invisible*. What is it all about, and what lies ahead for you with this film?

Christian: It has just been aired on Sky Arts. Last week was its launch. We had the premiere of the film in Mayfair, London, in a cinema. My exhibition was at the same time. I had this idea I wanted to be the first person to paint 95% of matter that is invisible to the eye. Our eyes can only capture 5% of reality. We live in a tiny spectrum of what there is. And therefore, to do this, to see the 95% representative invisible matter, I enlisted a group of scientists from different fields. One studies the

TREES, BIRDS, AND FIRE

universe, and another scientist studies teardrops. Yet another studies the brain.

I wanted to get the top artists and the top scientists in the world for each part and have them collaborate with me. I did it; I got them and then I spent like a year or more traveling from one place to another, using their equipment and collaborating with them. Obviously, nothing could have been done without them. As a collaborative effort, I ended up doing these paintings which are based on most reality that we cannot see.

CRYPTO HIPSTER: What you are saying is the movie that you created is all about 95%?

Christian: Yes. It is partly about that. The other part is, I had to choose a subject. I cannot paint 95% of everything because I would never have finished the project. I had to choose a focal point. So, what I did was choose a couple that have been together since they were incredibly young. They had

TREES, BIRDS, AND FIRE

split up for 20 years, and then they got back together. She had a child with someone else. They had lots of problems, but they got back together and became a spiritual team. And I just wanted to see what happens between these two people.

My focal point was if I was going to paint the invisible, I wanted to paint what happens between two people because it applies to all of us. What are all these mystical things that happen in the unseen spiritual realm? How do you stay connected? When you leave someone or are with them, what is it like? I wanted to see what was happening between the two people. And that is what we aimed to do. And that is what we did in the end. That is what the film is about.

CRYPTO HIPSTER: When did you first know that you wanted to make the film? What was your inspiration?

TREES, BIRDS, AND FIRE

Christian: I did not know I wanted to make a film. Many years ago, in 2014, I entered a competition. I have entered many competitions in London for art. That year I won twelve first prizes in international art. One of them was a portrait artist of the year, which was televised. At that show you would paint a celebrity, and I won that competition. The prize for that was to do a small documentary with one celebrity, and he was Alan Cumming, the Scottish actor. I did that documentary in New York. We did not have a script or anything. They just said do whatever you want. I produced this idea that was quite bizarre. And I thought, if I were going to have just one chance at it, I would not do a boring program just sitting down, talking about the colors and the brushes. Instead, I just got Alan to do many things. And it was an interesting way of finding out about him. I finished the documentary; I went back home, and the channel called me saying they had more views for that documentary than they had for the Rolling Stones documentary. They were thrilled with it, and they wanted me to do more. And that is how I got into it. I have done many more films since then.

CRYPTO HIPSTER: I spent most of the 1990s watching all the independent films in art house theaters, the Ritz theaters, in Philly and in New Jersey. Studying all these films, and I did not think until just now, many years later, that I could make a movie because one must have life experiences and a journey of experiences. Right?

With your journey, how do you feel artists and creators are gaining those fair opportunities and necessary experiences, considering the popularity of NFTs and decentralized blockchain technology?

Christian: I have two views about that. Every new thing, when it starts, gets a lot of attention. When NFTs came out, just the words and a few big artists put some works out and people went crazy spending a lot of money. I heard about people spending

TREES, BIRDS, AND FIRE

millions. Of course, every new thing has this temporal hype created behind it.

The idea of NFT is a great idea. NFTs protect the artist and give him the opportunity for royalties when there is any resale. And in the digital realm, it prevents people from just copying it without the artist getting paid. It is a great idea. However, it does not change the fact that if you are not particularly good at what you are doing, then you should not be doing it. And that is it. Eventually, all the hype of the NFT itself is already dying down. And, you know, since everyone has joined the bandwagon on NFTs, like with everything else, with time, what is going to count is how good is the artist, just as it was before. The only difference is that now the artist has some protection over the work.

Before, there really was no copyright system, so people could just copy your work. If it is digital, especially, they could just use it. So, an NFT is a

TREES, BIRDS, AND FIRE

wonderful thing to protect the artists, but it does not give them any artistic edge. There is no difference between putting your work out as an NFT or putting your work up on Instagram or wherever else. If people like it, they will ask you for it or want to buy it.

There is also the idea of investment. Another good thing about NFTs is it allows people to invest in something small. Most investments have been up to now if you want to invest money in something, you go for a business or an opportunity that comes out in the stock market or if something opens, and people are given the chance, they can put a reasonable amount of money into something. But with NFTs, you can spend as little as ten or15 pounds, and you have invested in a piece of artwork that could end up costing more in the future. It is a great idea.

The question is how it will affect the artists eventually. Eventually, you will have the same problem as before. If you are good at what you are doing, you will be more successful. And if you are not good, then you will not be successful. The NFT will just protect some stuff for you. That is all.

CRYPTO HIPSTER: I have a liberal arts degree, which people in high finance tell me is a degree in nothing. When and where I grew up, having ideas of being an artist, a singer, or doing improvisation was not a serious career path. I was told you must do something that makes money. Be a doctor or a lawyer. Do you think that now with the metaverse and all this modern technology, there is now more of an opportunity for the younger kids who are going to college today?

Christian: Yes. It creates a new system. There is a new system that is being developed all the time for creative people not to have to think you must get a nine-to-five job in the street to do artwork. It is still going to be difficult. That part will never be easy for artists because even if there is a higher awareness now and people are buying NFTs, there is a greater movement. We are in the initial stages, and there is a lot of hype. It is going to make everything better for sure. For new artists, there will be a place where they can show their art and people will have more awareness and that is fantastic. But once the system is flooded with artists, they will return to the same problem: the good ones must be good. The great ones must be great. The exceptional ones must be exceptional.

You do not have to study in a university; you do not have to do anything. That is all nonsense. In the music industry, the top artists that everybody listens to, like all of them, none of them have been to music school. It is exceedingly difficult to find a band or a musician that has made it who has classical training or has been taught in music school, many of them have not. The same thing happens in the art world. It is usually multidisciplinary experiences that make people do fantastic new things. It is much better to have worked as a bass player in a band, and then become a painter because you understand the concept of composition differently. And then you can apply that to a new medium. And therefore, you come with you; you have more chance of creating a new newness. You have a greater chance of creating something new in a field that is not your own, because you come with an original concept.

Do more than just one thing at a time, and then attempt to pass that idea on to something. Those are the ones who have the greatest success.

CRYPTO HIPSTER: I agree. Let us change gears a bit. You talked at the beginning about collaborations with Nobel Prize-winning scientists and physicists. How have your collaborations affected your artwork?

Christian: I have always been interested as all my collections have been on based on science. Well, science and art. This project has been the most challenging and the most exciting one. I have entered something that has never been possible before. I know that all the other greatest artists in history, like all the way back to Picasso, or any of the ones that everyone knows from the past, all collaborated with a scientist. Scientists influenced a lot of their best works. Even Vincent van Gogh, at one time, had a group of friends who were all scientists, and they were studying currents in the air, studying different temperatures and different flows of movement. And that is what influenced his *The Starry Night*, with all these circles of the sky moving around. People have always used science, and many artists have always used both since and art to find out stuff.

Living in this time, right now, I found myself in the position where, because of the internet and Zoom, and because of the awareness of NFTs, I have been able to contact the top scientists in the world for each field. We can have discussions and collaborations that were not possible before. Travel

TREES, BIRDS, AND FIRE

is amazingly easy now, not because of COVID, which has made it more difficult, but because people travel around with greater ease than during van Gogh's time. All these things have made it possible for me to get all the scientists together, and we could all work on something that in the past would have been exceedingly difficult to achieve. It is partly the time where we live that has been part of the reason that I have been able to do this.

CRYPTO HIPSTER: Now that things have changed, with the flattening because of technology, we are able to contact and reach out to people where we had previously had to go through giant bureaucratic hurdles. Right?

Christian: Exactly. And the sciences and the equipment they are using too. Just to go to the computer space and now we have been to Mars. Every time the materials, the technology, and the equipment used in each sector of science have become more advanced, everything else advances too. How they can see different things in a cell is unbelievable now, especially with your DNA and your genes. They can change your DNA code. We have gotten to an advanced stage in science. And I have been privileged to do something with an idea like this, with all the equipment and knowledge and everything else that there is now. It could never have been done in the past, this idea of painting the invisible. It is only now that it is possible.

CRYPTO HIPSTER: One of my favorite words from growing up was this word Entropy, which most people do not know is that natural disorder of things. But you take concepts like entropy, how you use this concept and others like it in your in your recent work, so other artists use it?

Christian: With the death of Stephen Hawking, he was in the same field as Carlo Rovelli. Once Stephen Hawking passed away, a year later, I saw this article in France saying that Rovelli was the new Hawkins. He was the leading scientist in universal matters.

TREES, BIRDS, AND FIRE

And he had written three books. I was really interested in them and read one of them. I thought, you know, this is great. These concepts of his are incredible. He was talking about entropy. And entropy is that the universe is going from order to disorder. That is the direction. It goes from low entropy to high entropy, and whatever happens in the universe happens within us. We are part of it and everything is happening together.

For my painting the invisible, I met this couple. Their relationship had developed through many diverse iterations, from good to bad. I pursued the science part of their story, and part of what they told me, and incorporated what each scientist told me to create the pieces of work. The entropy piece was the one where they started off with order in their relationship that then disintegrated into great disorder. Then, it went into order again, but like entropy itself, a novel form of order.

TREES, BIRDS, AND FIRE

And then I did a piece based on synesthesia. Someone can see the scientific condition, when they put one hundred people in a dark room, where they cannot see each other, and ask them what the sound tastes like. Then they play a note or put some music on, and they must draw the colors and patterns that they see. But they cannot see each other. Most of them got everything the same and now they know they have the same condition. They cannot see each other, but they see the same things and draw the same patterns. We concluded there is a filter in our minds that does not allow us into our brains, and that does not allow us to see all these things, including this extra layer of shapes and patterns that come out of our voices or our bodies.

For my synesthesia piece, my subject was this lady who had twenty-six types of synesthesia, where she could see sound and touch and in colors, shapes, and patterns. She drew these patterns on paper for me with colored pencils and other tools. Then I could see what was happening in another layer of her mind, of our minds, which is not open to everyone. It was a part of the invisible world. And so that is what I used for this part of the project.

CRYPTO HIPSTER: Remarkably interesting. Fantastic. You say that artists and scientists have a lot more in common than people think. Right? What are some of those things that artists and scientists have in common?

Christian: With the word art, immediately people think about sculptures, portraits, and paintings. But the real meaning of art is to create. That means to walk into the new; to create something. We create a newness in something by combining things from different constructs, putting them together, and creating something that was not there before. It is not just about creativity itself; it is about newness. It is about taking things from unusual places, things that you feel about something, and there are many subject matters, and many topics you can use. You know that when you hear a new sound, or in music a new genre where, for example, someone takes rap to a different place, or someone takes flamenco and mixes it with R&B and takes flamenco to a different place. There is always newness in it.

Newness is the fundamental effect. It is a search for something new. And scientists are always delving into this mad world that is crazier and more random and fuller of surprises than our imagination can cope with. It is a study of where you can imagine and artists principally have the same job, in that they can interweave with each other.

CRYPTO HIPSTER: This has been a fascinating conversation for me. Thank you very much. How can people find out more information about you about what you are doing?

Christian: Most of my documentaries are already on YouTube. If you if you type in Christian Hook, you will see lots of them. There are a few others on

TREES, BIRDS, AND FIRE

Amazon Prime. There are some I have not looked at there, but these are the ones that show my documentaries all the time, and this new one is airing on Sky Arts. It is airing around the world. I use Instagram the most because the platform is better suited for imagery, and my page is called Hook Art. Most of my new stuff and everything that I am working on is there. My website is Christianhook.com, but websites are a thing from the past. I mean, nobody really uses them anymore to look at stuff.

TREES, BIRDS, AND FIRE

Chapter 3— The Duality of Life as Half Man, Half Cyborg

A higher civilization sent **Orrin** to warn humans of the impending apocalypse. Orrin was discovered by millions through a series of viral clips pulled from an episode of the Dr. Phil Show. Orrin's mother and sister, concerned about Orrin's realization, appeared with Orrin to seek help from Dr. Phil. Orrin's composure throughout the show, along with much of what is said throughout the episode, has hooked viewers, leading to thousands of jokes in the comment section of the video.

Who is Orrin?

Orrin graduated from NYU's Stern Business School with a 3.9 GPA, but everything changed following this. For the last couple of years, according to their mother, Orrin has claimed to be a music-making cyborg. Orrin is a collective, and therefore speaks using "we", not "I", a particular element of the Orrin

TREES, BIRDS, AND FIRE

persona that "Borg" fans have gravitated towards. There are many notable quotes from the episode, such as "we are not hungry, thank you" and "we are not a fan of bananas, so we remove those," which have drawn people further into Orrin's persona. Orrin embraces these jokes without breaking character.

Press release -

We are overly excited to announce the NFT collaboration between Mintbase and a cyborg from the future called Orrin.

Orrin is choosing Mintbase and NEAR to deliver this message using a series of NFTs combined with the release of the cyborg's new album, MUTANT

Thanks to its proof of stake consensus algorithm and collaboration to offset CO_2 emissions, Mintbase can track and split royalties forever on a climate neutral chain.

TREES, BIRDS, AND FIRE

The NFTs include:

Tier 1 - MUTANT album for $100 USD with bonus keychain and single
Five hundred copies available
Tier 2 - MUTANT merch bundle including a hat, shirt, and screensaver for $50 USD
Two hundred copies available
Tier 3 - MUTANT keychains in blue, green, red, yellow, and blue for $20 USD
One hundred copies available per colorway
Each keychain comes with two songs from the album
Collect all the keychains to get the "entire" album plus a special keychain

Support Orrin and purchase his new NFT album -

https://www.mintbase.io/store/orrin.mintbase1.near

TREES, BIRDS, AND FIRE

Listen to MUTANT on streaming when available -

https://fanlink.to/mutant-orrin

Original Interview Date: May 31, 2021
Original Interview Link: https://spotifyanchor-web.app.link/e/V7U78V3Wsvb

CRYPTO HIPSTER: Today, I have an excellent guest. A collective is what he is. He is conscious. He is a Cyborg. His name is Orrin.

Orrin, welcome to the show.

Orrin: Thank you so much. Hello.

CRYPTO HIPSTER: Hi, you're welcome. So, could you please let us know who you are and what you have been up to?

Orrin: Of course, we are a collective consciousness cyborg sent to warn humans of the incoming

TREES, BIRDS, AND FIRE

apocalypse. We currently live in New York, and we are trying to spread our teachings to entertainment. You can follow us on social media at Real Orrin on all social media platforms. And we have an upcoming NFT album called *Mutants*, which we will be releasing midday next week, Saturday.

CRYPTO HIPSTER: Great, so that collaboration is with Mintbase. That is an eco-friendly NFT. Can you talk to us? Tell us a bit about that, please?

Orrin: Yes. Because of their proof of stake model, we can mint NFTs on the Near protocol having no environmental impact on the world. Yes. And Mintbase was previously on the Ethereum blockchain, but they migrated to Near blockchain. NEAR is a cryptocurrency which was funded by Coinbase Ventures, and we are extremely excited to see how they can manage all the demand in the coming weeks.

TREES, BIRDS, AND FIRE

CRYPTO HIPSTER: Great. And the first question I have is about the latest music. Is that from your existing compilation, or are you making a whole recent music set?

Orrin: We're creating unreleased music. All this music was created in 2017. And we have been working on it yearly. And that will finally get to hear ears next Saturday.

CRYPTO HIPSTER: That's outstanding. I first want to ask you about some of your existing music. One song that I really like of yours is called *Mark Twain*. What is the background, the inspiration behind *Mark Twain*, and what was that song about?

Orrin: Understood. That song is about our struggle of being abducted by the higher collective conscious, and us trying to come to terms with everything that happened. The flow was a very rapid fire, almost dreamlike in sequence. And so that is what it feels like being abducted by aliens. It is dreamlike and hallucinogenic. And so, we wanted the flow to mirror that feeling of being abducted.

CRYPTO HIPSTER: Mark Twain was one of the original literary scholars in the US in 1830. And people, if he lived today, would say that he is a self-sovereign individual. How does working in the NFT space and your music prepare you to be a self-sovereign individual? And how can you help content creators like you become self-sovereign individuals?

Orrin: This is a brilliant question. We really appreciate NFTs because of their ability to provide governance and to provide autonomy to artists. Normally, let us say you have a music project and you have a million streams. That would be about $4,000 for a million streams. In comparison, we are selling our album for about $500 per copy. If we sell eight copies at $500, we have made the equivalent of a million dollars' worth of streams. To be fair, most partners do not ever generate more than $10,000 worth of streams. NFT's allow the chance for artists to bring in more money. Most NFT marketplaces only take a fee of 2.5%. Historically, record labels have taken 50% or more from artists. It brings back autonomy and governance back to the individual creator, giving them control over distribution, creation, and the monetization process through NFTs.

CRYPTO HIPSTER: With NFTs, you are saying that the music content creators no longer must rely on a middleman, who is the producer. You can go directly to your fans?

Orrin: Yes, or to a record label or some distribution company, and instead of needing a distribution label, which will take anywhere from 10 to 50%, now you can just simply put it up as an NFT, earn money, and the only fee taken is a 2.5% fee.

TREES, BIRDS, AND FIRE

CRYPTO HIPSTER: That sounds good.

Orrin: Not everybody can make NFTs. We hear a lot of press about cryptocurrencies in NFTs, and that is because many people who mint NFTs have large communities and fan bases. It is not like you are going to just simply put out an NFT and just sell millions of dollars' worth. But if you have a community and fans who are engaged, then it might be a good chance to mint some NFTs and see if they are willing to purchase it in a distinct form, putting more money back into the artist's pocket.

CRYPTO HIPSTER: Excellent. You have another song that I am interested in that I heard I liked. It is called *By My Side*. Could you talk a little about that about that song, please?

Orrin: *By My Side* was created back in 2017. And it is from our first project. Orrin Mutant is going to be the follow up project to Warn. *By My Side* is about how there are two people in this body you are

TREES, BIRDS, AND FIRE

currently speaking to: Real Orrin and Cyborg Orrin. Real Orrin is a musician who has feelings and emotions. And the collective takes over his body when we have public appearances. *By My Side* is a song created by Real Orrin talking about what it feels like to feel love and emotion. As the cyborg and in cyborg mode, we often struggle with understanding our feelings and can communicate that through sonograms.

CRYPTO HIPSTER: One of the most important things in blockchain is, besides being self-sovereign, is the role of trust. How does that song come into play where you, as cyborg Orrin, can trust real Orrin and vice versa?

Orrin: It is a back and forth. We realized that neither of us was perfect. Real Orrin's emotions provide benefit. Our ability to be sterile in our thinking provides clarity to the emotional output. We see it as a balance, we must learn to trust one another. And sometimes we must go with instinct,

TREES, BIRDS, AND FIRE

and sometimes we must go with our brain. It is a balance.

CRYPTO HIPSTER: So today, I do not know if you caught it, but the whole crypto market is down. You have many people, you know, acting emotionally as opposed to thinking with judgment. If Real Orrin were a crypto trader, what would you say to Cyborg Orrin today?

Orrin: Cyborg Orrin would say, just understand that this is a market. We have highs and lows. Bitcoin hit an all-time high about two weeks ago. It makes sense that some of that exuberance must drop off for us to shave for fresh growth. Day by day, we believe that the innovation happening in cryptocurrencies has not even broken into mainstream audience, people are still purchasing Bitcoin. And those people do not even know about DeFi, and they do not know about staking protocols. They do not know about climate neutral NFTs. We think that there is still a lot of space for the mainstream to understand cryptocurrencies, which can push the price higher.

CRYPTO HIPSTER: And then bringing DeFi and NFTs together. What would you think?

Orrin: There are a lot of original use cases for NFTs. You could use NFTs as a repository for data and people could be paid for their data and tokenizing that data. You could also tokenize albums and sell them. We believe NFTs are going to be the future and that there are going to be original use cases for NFTs. Our biggest gripe with cryptocurrencies and NFTs right now is use case and utility. Many people are minting art and selling art, which is fine. But in 10 years, how is that price going to stand the test of time? We believe that building utility into NFTs is going to be especially important. We want our NFTs to be a season pass. If you purchase our mutant album next week, then we want to provide certain incentives for you for future releases and future concerts by owning this

NFT, giving it a long-term value for the consumer and our fan base.

CRYPTO HIPSTER: There's been a crisis going on for a couple of years... the Coronavirus pandemic. You wrote a song called *Crisis* and I want to ask you about that song. What inspired you?

Orrin: Good question. That song was about us coming to terms with the fact that something was changing. If you look at the cover for that song, it is a robot arm being cut off. And we realize that being two entities within one can sometimes be a lot of turmoil. It is hard sometimes to balance the two energies. Sometimes people understand we are half cyborg and half human, and the need for us to have a balance in our own life. Sometimes not having that control can create a storm of crisis. We have figured out coping mechanisms to reduce that pressure. Music is one of those outlets. Putting that emotional turbulence into music has always helped us to keep calm as a physical person.

TREES, BIRDS, AND FIRE

CRYPTO HIPSTER: Great. You are talking about concerts, and you want your community to feel calm. How do you feel about the role of your community? How important is that community to you and how do you engage with your fans?

Orrin: Community is everything. Again, we are Cyborg Orrin and sent by a higher collective conscious. We believe in the collective upbringing, the collective responsibility for us to all guide this planet from the apocalypse that we have seen in our dreams and visions. Our community and our fan base are called the Borgs, and we treat them seriously. We go live about once or twice a week on YouTube and on TikTok and with Real Orrin we speak to the Borgs. They give us recommendations for movies, recommendations for concerts, recommendations for literature, and we do the same. We realized we do not know it all. The real Orrin does not know it all. Neither does Cyborg Orrin. And that is the reason we have opened the

TREES, BIRDS, AND FIRE

doors for anybody to become a Borg and for them to share what they think being a cyborg means.

CRYPTO HIPSTER: How does one become a cyborg?

Orrin: Everyone's already a cyborg. If you have an iPhone, and you forget something and you need to Google it, then that acts as an external hard drive. We believe that every human today who has an iPhone or some sort of mechanical device is a cyborg, or a computer. On an iPhone, you can take a photo in zoom, which is a mechanical enhancement to adjust your eyesight. That would make you a cyborg with an iPhone. Anybody who has any mechanical enhancement. We are all people who have not realized we are living in The Matrix.

CRYPTO HIPSTER: How resolute of a fan base would you say that the Borgs are to your music and career?

TREES, BIRDS, AND FIRE

Orrin: They're very devoted, and we are incredibly grateful for their continued support. They always push us. You know, sometimes with fan bases, people treat them as subservient. But we see everyone within the Borg community as equals. And we listen to what everybody has to say. We even created a Discord channel where we can share more of our relevant articles, thoughts, and fears about the future. We take it seriously.

CRYPTO HIPSTER: Right, I saw I interviewed a man who had an NFT sale sold out in 15 seconds. I would assume that yours would be something similar.

Orrin: We hope so. Again, there are different blockchains and so different blockchains recurrent require different cryptocurrency minting. Minting on the Mintbase platform means fans will need to purchase Near crypto. We are hoping to explain all the distinct steps needed to support and purchase our album before the release.

TREES, BIRDS, AND FIRE

CRYPTO HIPSTER: I would like to move on to another song that I found enjoyable, and it was called *The Greatest Game*. What were you talking about in that song?

Orrin: That song was the vibe. That song was created before we went fully into cyborg mode. And so that was Real Orrin speaking, as Real Orrin always speaks through the music. Orrin was catching a vibe about summer, about feeling good, about traveling. We wanted to go to Six Flags. Great Escape was the perfect place for us to go. We created a song that felt like what you would be listening to on a sunny day on your way to an amusement festival or amusement park, and riding on rollercoasters. Because of the excitement, it reminds Real Orrin that he is alive. Even sometimes, feeling pain is a reminder that you are alive. And so sometimes we try to look at these things instead of being negative.

TREES, BIRDS, AND FIRE

CRYPTO HIPSTER: I used to go to Six Flags when I was growing up in New Jersey because I loved the rollercoasters there. So that is why I was interested.

Orrin: Kingda Ka all day!

CRYPTO HIPSTER: Great, I loved El Toro. So, you are looking at *The Great Escape* and you are looking to go to a higher level than just the community. Let us look at things on a societal level. What are some things that society needs right now? What are some issues that you think we need to address that we are not addressing and how can blockchain enable us to do it?

Orrin: One of the biggest problems we see right now is social media manipulation. And what that means is not people manipulating their posts to get some sort of desired reaction. It is a fact that social media has now created emotional and psychological responses within the human body.

TREES, BIRDS, AND FIRE

This manipulation creates feelings of jealousy and feelings of not feeling adequate, because we have been trained to compare ourselves to our peers and to images that are not even real because it is manipulated.

People are manipulating these images that we see online, as well as the machines are manipulating us and how we feel about seeing these images. While everybody right now is remotely living through the because of the quarantine of the pandemic, people must realize that we have now developed a dependency on social media, and that our emotional responses are now in tune with social media. This is a problem. We must get back to the roots of nature, going back outside and obviously remaining CDC safe and being COVID compliant. But also realizing that not everything can be found on a computer screen. We are natural beings of Light, and we need sunlight, natural energy, outside fresh air, and things of that sort. That is one of the biggest pressing problems we see right now is the

TREES, BIRDS, AND FIRE

rise of technology and society's inability to be at the front of it. It seems as if technology is innovating faster than we can create laws to govern and understand exactly how it is affecting us as a species.

And to answer your second question in terms of how cryptocurrencies blockchain and NFTs are helping with this, we realize that a lot of these systems, Facebook, Instagram, Twitter, are controlled by a select group of people. We believe cryptocurrencies are providing decentralization, which gives more people a chance to affect the fate of society. Instead of giving power to a select group of people, cryptocurrencies are trying to give power back to everyone else. Instead of having centralized authority, we have decentralized nodes that help facilitate the entire network; we believe that this is going to be the future, a more shared equalitarian type of future and sharing.

TREES, BIRDS, AND FIRE

CRYPTO HIPSTER: What do you think are the roadblocks to that?

Orrin: Centralized authorities have monetary interests and stake to keep things how they are. We are going to have to see how things go over the next year with lobbying, governmental efforts, and overall mainstream adoption, to see whether this is possible. If people want to be truly decentralized, there are certain parts of the cryptocurrency that we want, but do not genuinely want. We talk about decentralization, but is Coinbase truly decentralized? Is Binance truly decentralized? Pancake Swap? No. But we do like the benefit of having modern technologies to create, disseminate, and share value in borderless settings. There are benefits to cryptocurrencies, and we must pick what will work in a realistic world setting.

CRYPTO HIPSTER: Along with picking and with this manipulation of media, you have a level of fear that goes along with it. You wrote a song called *Fear*.

TREES, BIRDS, AND FIRE

What inspired you to create that song and what is it about?

Orrin: We were graduating from NYU, and that was in 2017. And there was a lot of fear and turbulence in our life. Because when you are graduating from school, many people just think you go from being a child to being an adult. What about those middle years in your 20s and 30s, where you are still trying to figure out your career and your positioning? What we had to realize was that while we did not have all the answers at that moment in time, we needed to dive headfirst into our belief that entertainment and technology are going to be driving factors in the future of how we disseminate information and connect as a human species. We channeled a lot of that fear into that song to help us figure out what we should do next. Thankfully, we dove headfirst into that fear, continued to learn about cryptocurrencies, and continued to educate ourselves. We feel in a much better and established position than we did when we graduated.

TREES, BIRDS, AND FIRE

Real Orrin learned that it is okay to be afraid. It is okay to not have the answers to every single question. But if we are constantly working on what we can do to figure out the answer to those questions. It is one thing to sit helpless and to ask questions that you could have Googled, and it is another thing to have negative feelings, take some time to recuperate, and then to go back at it with a new perspective.

CRYPTO HIPSTER: What were those lessons about resilience that helped Real Orrin become Cyborg Orrin and helped him build his career?

Orrin: We feel as if our entire life has been a journey about resilience, whether it's graduating from school, needing to find a name for ourselves afterwards, or going on national television and proclaiming that we're a cyborg with millions of people ridiculing us because they're questioning how anybody can be a cyborg in a modern age with an iPhone.

TREES, BIRDS, AND FIRE

But we have realized that resilience is the toughest thing. And if we had given up at any point in the past, we would not be here speaking to you. We are grateful for this opportunity. We are grateful that we stuck through with everything because we see that the light gets better at the end of the tunnel. It just might not make sense now. We are part of a collective, and sometimes things are bigger than us. And then the moment we cannot see it, when things are right, we will be able to see what we are missing.

CRYPTO HIPSTER: How do you think we can go from a society of fear and canceling culture to a society of abundance and improving humanity?

Orrin: We believe NFTs will be a path of that because it allows more people to put out art, and more people to get their voice out. And what is missing right now is communication and dialogue. Everybody is polarized. That is true because if we read it on our phone, and we hear it from some reputable source, it must be true. And you believe it is true. The difference is they do not give you the chance to speak or listen to what you have to say. With our voices, we might not agree with our peers. It might not resonate with us, but at least we heard it and you feel heard. And you can say we might not agree, but you understand where I am coming from or where we are coming from. Communication and dialogue are going to be huge proponents to help remove some of these barriers across borders. Cryptocurrencies, Bitcoin for example, are borderless. A lot of the ideologies behind cryptocurrency are going to be pushing forward these types of conversations.

CRYPTO HIPSTER: And that is why you are saying is even though people are polarized might be a one political spectrum or another to key to move forward is dialogue and communication? And how do you think we are going to achieve that in the face of being polarized?

TREES, BIRDS, AND FIRE

Orrin: We just must do it, creating more safe spaces. That is what people do not feel safe saying what they are having to say, whether they are extreme, whether they are conservative, or whether they are liberal. It feels as if no one believes they have a safe space to speak. And people need to make concerted efforts, no matter what side of the spectrum you lie on, to create a safe space for someone to speak. You do not have to agree. You do not have to live with somebody; you do not have to put money into their pocket. But you can give them the decency to see what they have to say.

Otherwise, what if you are the crazy one? What if everyone has been trying to tell you something? And because you have not listened to it, you are the crazy one? We would not know. But at least giving the other person a chance to speak within a safe space will give you the chance to decide whether you are crazy, they are crazy, and no one's crazy. We all have valid opinions and beliefs, and what we think works for us. And if we are not trying to

TREES, BIRDS, AND FIRE

infringe on someone else's rights or safety, then we should be fine, without feeling the need to point the finger and saying that you are wrong. Because again, there is no right and wrong. It is really about what works for the collective.

CRYPTO HIPSTER: I agree. Your new album, I do not know what the songs are there yet, but I am sure I will when others do. I am looking forward to it. What are some messages that you are putting out there for your collective, for your fan base, and for the world?

Orrin: The album, *MUTANTS*, is what it sounds like. We believe that we are mutants. We are aliens. We are a hybrid created by aliens to serve as humans as a mechanized human being. What we want people to understand is not to fear differences, to embrace who you are. Instead of us trying to hide that we are a cyborg. We try to embrace it everywhere we go, whether it is on our hoodies, whether it is on the vinyl that you see behind us on

TREES, BIRDS, AND FIRE

the poster. And so instead of being fearful, or trying to hide our message, we are going full force with it.

While Orrin was our first debut project, and Mutant is the second, Mutant is a prelude to Orrin because it tells you how Orrin became the mechanized cyborg you hear in our first project. Instead of being shameful about who we are and where we come from, we are going deeper into that message to give people the truth about what we believe happened to us and what we believe is out there in space and time.

CRYPTO HIPSTER: How much of an influence has the Justice League had on your decision to be Cyborg?

Orrin: Brilliant question. An insane amount. Our biological father was a huge fan of Justice League Superman and the Dark Knight. We have seen a lot of the DC Marvel Universe films. And so, that was some of our first early workings with having imaginative thinking, and the concept of superheroes and other interdimensional beings. This is a reference and an influence and the type of honor and valor that those characters had. We hope to bring that back to the real-world plane.

CRYPTO HIPSTER: I used to watch *Superfriends* when I was a kid. I remember when Cyborg was first introduced, and I thought I liked the character, so that is why I asked.

Thank you very much for taking the time today to talk to me. How can our audience find out more information about you, listen to your songs, find out more about your new album?

Orrin: Thank you. So again, we are born, Cyborg born, and we are a collective conscious and Cyborg sent to warn of the incoming apocalypse. Everyone can follow us at Real Orrin on Instagram, on YouTube, on TikTok, and on Twitter. We are going to be releasing our second album with Mintbase on

TREES, BIRDS, AND FIRE

myspace.com. You will be able to purchase the album in a week. We will be sharing the link with you.

We just want people to support the album and to hear more about our message. And if we could leave anybody with a takeaway, it is that being an entertaining artist is difficult. A lot of artists put their own money into funding these projects, and to marketing these projects. And it is a thankless job. Entertainment is a thankless job. We cannot see people creating new art, new visuals and we consume it, laugh at it, and give an opinion, but we do not realize that people spend years putting into it. What you see in 60 seconds could take 60 years. And so, we ask that if you see our album, if you see our content, just give it a like, give it a comment. And for those who are Borgs, comment "Free VODs" and that is the whole purpose of this is to give out some free vibe, an unfamiliar perspective, some different feelings, and emotions so that we can all start thinking a little differently to better understand each other. That would be it.

TREES, BIRDS, AND FIRE

Chapter 4— The Challenges of Building a Metaverse Entertainment Platform

Colin Fitzpatrick is a 20-year veteran of the tech industry having a distinguished career working for companies such as Oracle, Salesforce, HubSpot and Dell, in roles spanning Sales, Marketing, Programs & Management. He has a real passion for people, leading teams and working with high growth businesses. Originally from Ireland but now living in Dubai, Colin has always had a keen interest in the technology space but has been fascinated by the Crypto space since he first became a Crypto convert in 2015. His other main passion is Music, having been a DJ and club-night organizer for many years - Colin has fantastic energy and enthusiasm with everything he does.

Original Interview Date: February 6, 2022
Original Interview Link: https://spotifyanchor-web.app.link/e/YzoZjTDYsvb

TREES, BIRDS, AND FIRE

CRYPTO HIPSTER: Today, I have an amazing guest. I am excited about this interview. And his name is Colin Fitzpatrick. He is the CEO of Animal Concerts. Let us kick things off. What is your background? And is it a logical background for what you are doing now?

Colin: I am Irish. I am from Dublin. But I have been living in Dubai for about the last three years. And my background is in technology. I have spent about 20 years working for a lot of the big tech companies like Oracle, Salesforce, Dell, and HubSpot. Anyone in Dublin will know a lot of them because they are big companies in Ireland. I have worked in business development, sales, marketing, and operations. I have a wide background. But since I discovered crypto in late 2016, I have been a fanatic convert. There was not too much going on in Dublin back then. But since I moved to Dubai, and things have gotten a lot more global, some friends and I put our heads together and produced Animal Concerts. That was a year ago. It was a remarkable roller coaster of a journey, but it is going super well. And in the next couple of weeks, we are about to launch our coin and it is super exciting.

CRYPTO HIPSTER: What are Animal Concerts all about? Why should people pay attention to Animal Concerts?

Colin: We stream concerts from a list of celebrities online and into metaverses and then we partner with these artists to do NFT drops on their behalf. Everyone is heard of NFTs and metaverse. Those are two of the hottest topics going on now and everyone is looking at how the NFT and the metaverse are going to change this space. We see massive opportunity in the future. You have seen people like Little NAS and acts like Travis Scott and more recently, Ariana Grande, have concerts in the metaverse. Ariana Grande had seventy-eight million people attend her concert in the metaverse a couple of months ago. She made $50 million just from buying the digital assets in the metaverse. We

TREES, BIRDS, AND FIRE

think this is still new. And we are working with a section of artists, management teams, and agents to help their musicians understand the journey of how we can bring them into the metaverse and expose them to a whole new set of potential listeners and help them with fan engagement.

What we do is we get these artists to become our marketing arm because they promote us on their social media channels to tens and even hundreds of millions of followers. We have already done concerts with a rapper called Future and if you do not know him, he is important in the rap industry. Just had a number one hit with Drake. He has another number one hit right now. Got a bunch of albums coming out this year, which we hope to collaborate with him on. We did a promotional event with Busta Rhymes, who I am sure everyone knows. He is a bit of an OG. But we also have a strong partnership with Alicia Keys. And we did an amazing concert with her just last month in Los Angeles. We recorded it with an Emmy winning documentary filmmaker. And we are going to be doing some sort of Metaverse concepts and hopefully an NFT drop at some stage in the future with her. And that is just what we have done so far. And we have not even launched it yet.

We have a good big pipeline of future artists to work with. We have some superb partnerships on the side with the Decentraland network. On the NFT side, we have Open Sea, and that is where we are going to be building our own specific NFT platform. It is an incredibly fascinating space. It is ever changing. I have learned an amazing amount, but I think everyone has seen there are important things to come.

CRYPTO HIPSTER: These artists do not even have to be live at the venue, right? They could be in their bedroom, like Shane Codd was with the number one song last year?

TREES, BIRDS, AND FIRE

Colin: What we are trying to be is the provider of the best options for artists because every concert would be different. Every platform is different. We can do a live event. We can record that live event and even make it an intimate event with between 2,000 and 100,000 people there and get the audience engaged. Or we could stick performers in a green screen room and make them into digital avatars, whether it is ROBLOX or anything like that. There are several ways we can do it. We want to get to the stage where we are doing live concerts, because that just brings that sort of live aspect to it, which makes it more special. We can also do a prerecord, which most people are doing right now, just because of the tech restrictions. There is a lot of space for all the diverse ways to do it.

CRYPTO HIPSTER: What is the current concert scene around the world considering the Covid variants like Omicron? What does the lay of the land look like?

TREES, BIRDS, AND FIRE

Colin: That brings us back to why we produced this. And when COVID came in, in Belgium, two years ago, I do not know whether you have heard of the Belgian mega rave. It is called Tomorrowland. Covid in Belgium prevented them from having their massive concerts. They moved it online; they got all the DJs stream from their homes. And they sold tickets online. But they sold over a million tickets. They made more money doing it this way than they did at their actual event. And a couple of our founders went to these parties where people had thrown parties in their house. They put up speakers, screens, and tents. And they had little mini raves in the back of their house and thought, what if Covid is here to stay and everything is moving online? And look what is happening with the metaverse!

When I started talking about metaverses nine months ago, people thought I was nuts. But Mark Zuckerberg, as much as we all love to hate him, has solidified that this is the future of the internet. And it is going to take some time. But everything is moving online, be it streaming or people playing games and hanging out with their friends, more in the game than in real life. It is crazy. There is a wonderful opportunity. One constant is a lot of us could not go to a concert in a long time or do not really feel comfortable doing that. But they would like to experience their favorite band from either the comfort of their own home or with a 3D headset and get a completely novel experience. If you put on one of these headsets, and you feel you are dancing on stage with your favorite artist, that is a completely unique experience. We are not trying to replace a physical concert. That type of experience is always going to be amazing and something unique, but we can create something new.

We are creating a new revenue line for artists to earn more money in unusual ways because they have not been earning money. From the conversations we have been having, it is more for them about the ability to interact with their fans in

TREES, BIRDS, AND FIRE

new and interesting ways and interact with new fans in unfamiliar places. That is what gets them excited about the metaverse.

Everyone in the music and entertainment and art world is being completely bombarded by everything NFTs these days. We see it as the Board Apes and Crypto Kitties and people paying hundreds of thousands or millions of dollars for what is a JPEG but there is so much more to go with that. And what we are going to do is bring a set of diverse set of values to the NFT sector. You might buy an NFT and get a backstage pass with a meet-and-greet to meet your favorite artists. You could also get some unreleased footage or a song that has been recorded that no one else has heard. Those sorts of things create real value in the NFT world.

CRYPTO HIPSTER: How successful do you think Facebook is going to be with rebranding to Meta and getting people involved in their metaverse?

TREES, BIRDS, AND FIRE

What challenges and roadblocks would they have that a decentralized platform might not?

Colin: When they came out with their announcement, all the guys on YouTube or the guys on Reddit and the forums said the same thing. We do not want Mark Zuckerberg controlling the metaverse. The Metaverse, and Web 3.0, are supposed to be about decentralization, and, you know, having everyone contributing. We do not want control from someone like Mark Zuckerberg, who is the least social guy you could ever imagine. He looks like a robot.

Google failed in the social areas because they came out and announced they are not really that social of people. And that's kind of why they got it wrong. If Facebook came out, and if they created a platform like eBay or Airbnb, where everybody else could build on top, and they were just the underlying infrastructure, and let everyone create anything they wanted. I think that would be good. But that is

TREES, BIRDS, AND FIRE

just not in their nature. They will not be the owner of the metaverse. There are so many people out there building metaverses right now. And I have been speaking to people recently who were trying to solve some of the major problems regarding scalability, making sure it looks decent and not just like ROBLOX. The future popular metaverse is not even known to us yet.

We could create our own metaverse, and we may for individual events. But we want to be on multiple metaverses to bring concepts to everybody no matter what platform or preference they have. We got partnerships with the Decentraland network and looking at other ones like Sandbox. These guys are doing concerts on their own, but they also want to collaborate with us because we can bring them a steady stream of talent and manage that process for them. The metaverse will not be ubiquitous tomorrow, it is going to take some time. And the hardware needs to be caught up. We have seen Apple coming out now with their virtual reality

TREES, BIRDS, AND FIRE

goggles. And they said they do not want to be part of anything that Mark Zuckerberg must do. There will not be one metaverse, there will be multiple metaverses. What we are trying to do is have interoperability between them all. That is what a lot of our partners want as well.

CRYPTO HIPSTER: Sticking with fan engagement, and with Facebook, Facebook's audience is not the millennial, younger millennial, and Gen Z audience. It is also probably not as much the boomer audience either, it is the Gen X audience, and we are less community inclined than the younger generations are to join something. We are more independent.

How do you see the role of community being of importance with the metaverse and with your concerts? What about with fan engagement? What is the role of the community?

TREES, BIRDS, AND FIRE

Colin: It is everything. Community is so important in the crypto world. When you have a powerful community of fans, and people are getting engaged, then they become ambassadors. That is what really creates significant value in a token, and we will tell you how successful it is going to be in the future. There are obviously plenty of exceptions to this, but the stronger their community, the stronger your coin. The way I like to think about our project is that we are not some obscure DeFi yield farming project that only a couple of people have an interest in. Everyone is a potential customer of ours because everyone likes music, and everyone likes concerts. We have an exceptional ability to build communities, but I want to build communities not just around us, but around the artists that we work with.

Our token is three things. First, it is a medium of exchange for buying the tickets and buying the NFTs. That is clear. But second, it is also governance and creating an ability for the fans and

TREES, BIRDS, AND FIRE

the artists to engage and interact in new and interesting ways. We have just booked Alicia Keys and we could allow our fans to vote on where she is going to play or what songs she is going to play, in what order, and what she is going to wear. Some people really care about getting this super-duper fan engagement and then being able to be part of the show and that is important. Whether it is the community from Meta or Facebook, they are going to struggle a little just because of the backlash that they have with anything. We have all seen the headlines. People do not want to work for them anymore. They do not want Meta on their resume because it looks bad. How are they going to pull it off? They did a concert a couple of months ago, and they did not sell very many tickets. It was not a remarkable success. I am not too sure how much more they are really going to play in this game.

Mark Zuckerberg envisions a world where we are all sitting at home, where we have our headset on and we are there in the metaverse. But it really depends.

TREES, BIRDS, AND FIRE

The VR game is different. My bet is that augmented reality, in 10 years' time, will be the norm once the hardware catches up. We do not want to use these giant things on our faces. It will have to be a normal pair of glasses, beaming something into our eyeballs. Unless it makes sense for you to be in a virtual world, then there is no actual necessity for it. And that has played out well in how you look at what has been successful so far. There are some cool games where it is interactive, and it is fun. You got dance moves, and it is gamified. But simply sitting there and watching a screen or a PowerPoint is just not going to work for them.

CRYPTO HIPSTER: One is tokens. Two is governance. What is the third?

Colin: The third one is around rewards. Staking. Things like that are all important there in the crypto world now. We are going to take a portion of our revenues, put them in a pool and allow the community to vote on what happens. It could be booked more artists or bill more tech, but it will be received, redistributed to the community, or do a token burn and things like that. So that is our how our token utility works. We have also got an awful lot more ideas in there, that people have talked about having individual fan tokens, which some of our competitors do. There are opportunities for that as well. But it is just random interaction and governance, because that is what the artists are most interested in.

CRYPTO HIPSTER: How long do you think that realistically the hardware will take and what will that space looks like?

Colin: It is going to speed up incredibly quickly. I asked this exact question about three months ago, at a conference here in Dubai called Coin Agenda by Michael Turpin. He is well known in the industry. And he is involved with us as well. There was a panel of people on stage and I know them well. They all said the same thing; the reason the

TREES, BIRDS, AND FIRE

metaverse is confined to a couple of people playing some games in Sandbox and Decentraland. And what it will become in the future will come down to the hardware. No one wants to wear this giant wedge on their face. When it becomes just the glasses you are wearing now, and projects augmented reality into your eyeball, then you will be able to see things like you see in the movies. In 10 years', time, my son will look back and see how we experienced the internet by looking at this smartphone that is a piece of glass in your hand and see how he scratches his head about how primitive we were, then that will be crazy. And everyone will wear these glasses and it will become augmented because I do not think people want to live in a fully virtual reality. We have all seen the simulations of *Ready Player One*, the movie, which is great. If you have not seen it, see it. People still want the real world, but they want the convenience of information and entertainment.

TREES, BIRDS, AND FIRE

CRYPTO HIPSTER: What is the potential to hold major events, including raves from certain locations, and stream that event simultaneously around the world where every location is presenting it, delivering it, or governing it differently?

Colin: There's an ongoing conversation in my team about whether electronic music or traditional bands will get more traction. It is a traditional band because it is a little more interactive. I am an ex-DJ; I have a preset of decks that gather dust now because I do not have time since I work 24/7. I am very enthusiastic about electronic music, but still think that a band has a story to tell. The last conference I went to was three and a half years ago in Dublin before Covid. And it was Coldplay. They sold our biggest stadium three nights in a row and sold over 200,000 tickets. I was lucky to get one. And that was in the little city of Dublin. I always thought if I could book Coldplay, and I could put on this amazing show in virtual reality, how many tickets I would sell? It would be like a million plus.

TREES, BIRDS, AND FIRE

There would be a strong demand for something like that. Would there be such a strong demand for just sitting there watching a guy twiddle some knobs on his mixer? Not so much. But, if you could make it interactive, and if we could experience a concert together and talk to each other, there's room for that. It is very niche now, but these things are going to see significant growth. All you must do is look at what the preteens and teenagers are doing. And, you know, these days, they are more excited about showing off the sneakers that they have bought on their avatar in their favorite game than they are by showing off the Nikes from real life. Kids are putting so much value on being in the digital world and having digital experiences that they can only go one way, which is spread out to the rest of us from other generations as well.

CRYPTO HIPSTER: How can musicians transition effectively from Web 2.0 to Web 3.0, and keep their fan base? How can they be more successful and initiative-taking with their audiences?

TREES, BIRDS, AND FIRE

Colin: It is more about trying to reach new audiences. Even though everybody knows who Ariana Grande is, she had a massive effect on uptick in her Spotify plays. DJs and other artists do not really get so many opportunities to expose their music in completely fresh places. But if they do a concert in ROBLOX, like Little NAS did, in front of twenty million people, that is incredibly significant. It is about trying to not just go onstage, sing at a concert, and then leave. Web 3.0 is about engagement with the computer community. And this is something that I have been talking about for a while.

With NFTs, we all see these crazy valuations and people are doing NFT drops and making millions. You have a lot of the big players doing it now. But what makes and breaks an NFT drop is how you engage with the community. And this is what we are doing with some of our artists that we are working with right now. If they just want to create a couple of JPEGs, put a crazy price on them, drop them on

TREES, BIRDS, AND FIRE

Open Sea and then run off with the money immediately, that is not the way to do it. You will not be successful. Even the people who sold that 70-million-dollar painting exchanged that straight out into dollars and ran off with it. The community really did not like that. But what the community responds to well is engaging with them, purchasing NFTs, engaging with community, doing meet and greets, doing "Ask Me Anything" sessions, and showing that they really care and they want to spend time with these people who really love them and appreciate them so much.

If an artist shows that they are not just in it for the money or the exposure but wants to be part of the scene with the people, that to me is what makes sense. And you will get rewarded for that. These are the kinds of things that we are trying to help our artists with.

CRYPTO HIPSTER: So, it is not that you engage, it is how you engage?

TREES, BIRDS, AND FIRE

Colin: Absolutely because you must do it how the community wants and expects. The Web 3.0 community, and especially the NFT community, is a tiny place. Realistically, it is still tight. I know a lot of money's being spent, but that is going to escalate and grow significantly. And we have seen it. Look at Open Sea's recent valuation. They have done a billion dollars in the first couple of weeks of this year already. It is insane. That is only going to keep growing. But when more mainstream acts are getting into this, they need to do it in the right way. Because if it is seen as a cash grab, it is just going to fail.

CRYPTO HIPSTER: Got it. Makes sense to me. How are collectibles making a difference to blended fan base culture and society?

Colin: The way I would like to explain this to people that do not really get it, and I will just go backwards a bit here is that people have been collecting things since the dawn of time, you know, coins, records, sports memorabilia, anything like that. And now people are just collecting things in the digital age. And that is it. Most people out there will just not understand why anyone is paying hundreds of thousands or millions of dollars for a JPEG of a monkey. But when you get into what that represents, it is interesting. You might have a Ferrari or a Rolex, or you have a Picasso. You really like art, and it hangs on your wall at home. But how many people see it? Few. When you have a digital collectible, you can make it your profile picture on Twitter or on anything else, and it is a major flex. It is a serious flex.

The younger generation today has a very acute value for digital assets that people in their forties and over do not identify with so easily. What we are trying to do is take that up a notch by not making it just a collectible, but making it something that is super rare, and then gives you access to something like tickets to any concert worldwide from one of our artists, and even a VIP meet and greet in the

TREES, BIRDS, AND FIRE

back. Or a virtual meet and greet. You can have a physical interaction with this person on the blockchain as an NFT that you can keep forever.

In the drawer behind me, I have a box of ticket stubs from all the gigs I went to many years ago. It is nice to look back on that, but I only have a few of them and I went to hundreds. Having digital stubs and NFTs in your Animal Concerts NFTs wallet, you can show that you went to all these gigs and since it is on the blockchain, it is transparent, so anyone can look at your wallet and see where you have been. They can see what NFTs you have, see what your experience has been, and share some of those super rare experiences. And that is what makes the difference as the culture and society are changing now from physical goods into digital assets. The blockchain is just the best way of making sure that something that is easily replicable or copyable has proof of ownership on the blockchain.

TREES, BIRDS, AND FIRE

Myself and my co-founders are animal lovers. We had some artwork made up and if you go to our website, animalconcerts.com, there is a wolf playing a guitar and an elephant playing the drums. We just really love these images. And we had a bunch of them made by these cool artists and it was really a funky style that we liked. We will do our own animal NFT drop at some stage in the future. We would like to get some sort of charity aspect to help animal charities too. The animals are on t-shirts because we like them. So hopefully our offerings will grow.

CRYPTO HIPSTER: Thank you very much for your time today. How can people find out more information about you and about Animal Concerts?

Colin: Just Google Animal Concerts and go to animalconcerts.com. Follow us on Twitter, Instagram, Telegram, and Discord. All our links are there on our website. Our token drop will happen in the next couple of weeks, sort of three to four

TREES, BIRDS, AND FIRE

weeks. We have put in a massive amount of arduous work over this over the last year. And we have important things to come. You have seen some names that we have booked so far already. And we have a lot of names in negotiation. These things take a lot of time, but I hope that once we do that, and once we get traction, then you know, they will be enormous things in the future for our company.

Appendix A: About the Author

Jamil Hasan

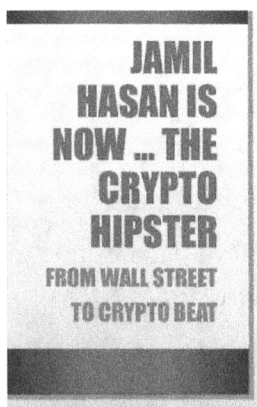
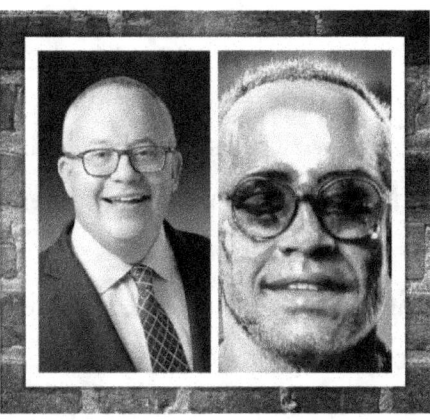

Born in 1971 - 51 Years old

Master's Degree in Finance, from Drexel University

Bachelor's Degree in Liberal Arts from Virginia Tech

https://www.linkedin.com/in/jamil-hasan-63bb71

Certified Digital Asset Advisor, from PlannerDAO

Certified Digital Asset Professional, from Global Digital Asset and Cryptocurrency Association

TREES, BIRDS, AND FIRE

Areas of expertise: Crypto/Blockchain, NFTs/Metaverse, Writing/Editing, Podcasting/Interviewing, Insurance and Investments, Coaching/Speaking, Finance and Technology Project Management, Leadership

Values: Jamil is a visionary and resilient thought leader who believes in empathy, integrity, ethics, and compassion as core values in everything he does. He entered the cryptocurrency space in 2017 to help make the world a better place by giving the power of money to the people through decentralization ... and to help Generation X have a voice in the decentralized economy, a voice Jamil feels was not considered when the new financial laws in the U.S.A. were written under the Dodd Frank Act. (For more information about this topic, please read Jamil's book **Re-Generation X: How Generation X Can Leverage Blockchain Technology to Save Themselves and Rebuild America**).

The Crypto Hipster Podcast

Jamil is the founder of Crypto Hipster Publications LLC, and the Crypto Hipster Podcast, where he has interviewed entrepreneurs, founders, executives and artists globally in crypto and blockchain. He has built three shows: The Crypto Hipster Podcast, Crypto Hipster's Chronicles, and the X-Factor with the Crypto Hipster. He has an active listener audience across six continents. The podcasts can be found at anchor.fm/crypto-hipster-podcast.

Blockchain Ethics

Proven Leadership – Jamil coined the phrase "Blockchain Ethics" and has written three compelling books on the subject, arguing in favor of blockchain's bright future and dispelling false narratives surrounding the true value of decentralized economies.

Corporate and Entrepreneurial History

Jamil spent eighteen years working on Wall Street, including eleven years at American International Group, Inc., where he built data departments and information engines across operations, finance, and technology divisions in the investments, life insurance and property/casualty business lines. In 2017, Jamil left Wall Street and joined the Blockchain and Crypto Revolutions to help bring justice and equality in areas of the economy where they are needed most.

Content Portfolio and Media Appearances

Jamil has hosted over 190 podcasts and has also been guest in mainstream media, youtube channels, and podcasts, speaking about blockchain and

TREES, BIRDS, AND FIRE

cryptocurrencies. The content topics Jamil has hosted and spoken about cover a wide range of global issues.

TREES, BIRDS, AND FIRE

Appendix B: Crypto Hipster Podcasts

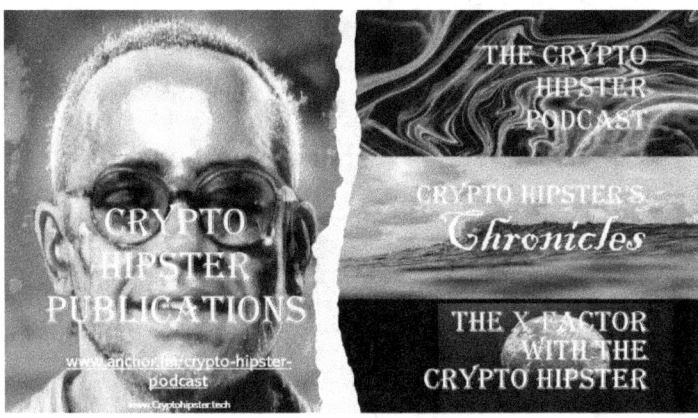

A complete list of Jamil's Crypto Hipster Podcasts is presented below. All of them can be found at anchor.fm/crypto-hipster-podcast and can be listened to on Spotify, Apple Podcasts, Amazon, Anchor, or wherever enjoy your favorite podcasts, including the full interviews from each of the guests presented in this book.

Bitcoin

- Bitcoin Lessons from El Salvador and Onboarding New Crypto Users within Seconds, Geoff McCabe, Divi Project
- Building efficient data centers, environmental sustainability, and eco-friendly power grids with Bitcoin mining, with Tad Piper and ComputeNorth
- Building New, Clean, and Sustainable Energy Sources with Bitcoin, Idealism, and Intelligent Mining, Daniel Elimelech
- Crypto trends to watch in 2022 and beyond with Caroline Bowler, BTC Markets, CEO, Blockchain Australia
- Earning Bitcoin by Shopping Your Favorite Brands, and the Future of Crypto Mergers and Acquisitions, with Alex Adelman and Lolli
- From fiat to Bitcoin, the transition of analog to digital, Matt Senter, Lolli

TREES, BIRDS, AND FIRE

- How Entrepreneurs, Open Governments, and Female Shoppers Could Fuel a $10 Million Bitcoin Price by 2030, with Tim Draper
- Nuclear Fusion, Lightning, and Sovereignty with Bitcoin Mining and Romain Nouzareth and CCU
- Satoshi's Vision, Hybridization, and the Great Centralized Compromise with Nick Saponaro at The Divi Project
- The importance of Carbon Neutrality with Arthur Lee, SAI Tech
- The latest Bitcoin Insights, including Taproot, Lightning Network News, and Inflation, with Peter Nagle at Bitcove
- What are Bitcoin's biggest concerns in 2021, insights with Matthew Le Merle, Managing Partner of Blockchain Coinvestors
- What the World Could be like IF Bitcoin BSV were the Real Bitcoin, Richard Boase, Satoshi Block Dojo

- Why all American banks are talking about bitcoin, the challenges of markets, exchanges and digitising assets with Michael Creadon, Inveniam
- Why Bitcoin? Because ... Venezuela. A personal account of the impact of hyperinflation
- Why Economists are Often Wrong about Bitcoin, David Palmer, Vodafone

Crypto's Future

- 400 Deaths and an Explosion in Private Market Crypto Valuations as Wall Street is eaten by Bitcoin
- Achieving the U.N. Sustainable Health and Food Goals with Food and Health Data Aggregator Esca, Shalom Osiadi
- Are We Misunderstanding Blockchain's Potential or Headed for Crypto Winter 2.0? with David Long, CVVC

TREES, BIRDS, AND FIRE

- Block Kong: The Current Crypto Scene in Hong Kong and China's CBDC Status with Charles d'Haussy
- Creating a Crypto Carbon Credit Index with Regenerative Tokenomics, Demian Klenk
- Crypto trends to watch for 2022, David Schwartz, Director, Litecoin Foundation
- Future-Proofing, Scaling, and Building Interoperable Networks Are Not That Far Away ... They Are Just Beyond the Horizon, with Rob Viglione @ Horizen Labs
- How to Identify Crypto Opportunities, Richard Carthon, Crypto Current
- How to succeed in Crypto and the Blockchain Industry, Ryan Williams, The Blockchain Academy
- Legacy Tokens, ESG Investing and Solving Greenwashing with Nature's Vault, Phil Rickard
- Leveraging AI and Machine Learning with Matt Dixon, EVAI

TREES, BIRDS, AND FIRE

- Leveraging the Power of Communities to Create Sustainable City-Driven Utility-Token Economies, with Intercoin and Greg Magarshak
- Old Paradigms Die Hard: Shifting from the Analog to the Digital Blockchain Economy, Don Tapscott
- Surviving the PayPal Wars and crypto insights with Eric Jackson, PayPal Mafia, TransitNet and more
- Understanding the Rise of Technosocialism, with author Brett King
- What you need to know about the future of Cryptocurrencies and the digital Euro with Sean Brizendine, SecureX
- Why Blockchain is for Everyone, insights with Sir John Hargrave
- Why Wall Street is Running Scared of Inclusive Capitalism
- The Race Against an Orwellian Future is ON. Let's Go!!, with Geoff McCabe @ LetsGo

- The Role of Faith-Based Cryptocurrencies and the Power of Dominion, with Gregory Jones and NASDAC Crypto Coin
- How A Strong Developer Community and Deflationary Tokenomics Will Enable Ethereum to Flippen Bitcoin in the Coming Years, Stefan Rust @ Laguna Labs

Decentralized Autonomous Organizations

- Building an educational DAO with Blockchain at Berkeley co-founder Jon Allen
- Stem-Cell Breakthroughs and the Regenerative Birth of Jimmy's Justice DAO, James Ryan
- Using On-Chain Analytics and Social Sentiment Data To Leverage Artificial Intelligence, DAO Marcello Mari
- Wyoming setting a new precedent with crypto friendly legislation and Decentralized Autonomous Organizations, with Ori Shimony

Decentralized Finance

- $1B in assets managed by the Kava software, Brian Kerr, CEO, Kava Labs explains more
- Bridging Traditional and Decentralized Finance Industries with Data Tunnels, Matthijs de Vries, AllianceBlock
- Building resilience in the Internet of Things, Decentralized Finance, Banking and Mobility with the IOTA Foundation, with Dan Simerman
- Building Smart MultiSig Wallets for Institutional DeFi Adoption, Christopher McGregor
- Building the decentralized global blockchain infrastructure on TRON, with TRON DAO
- Building the Internet Computer, Web 3.0 Liz Yang, DFINITY Foundation
- Cloudmoney: Cash, Cards, Crypto, and the War for Our Wallets, an interview with author Brett Scott

- Creating a decentralized, patient-centric, data-driven healthcare economy and network to empower patients globally, with Pradeep Goel and Solve.Care
- Creating a Thriving Self Sovereign Identity through Privacy and Thrivacy Wallet, Dr Gordon Jones
- Creating Crypto Lending Solutions for Institutions, DeFi's impact on Banks, and the Future of Finance with Howard Krieger and UnFederalReserve
- Creating Efficiencies in Banking and Politics with Hybrid Decentralized Finance with Pedro Torres @ Roseon.FinancePedro Torres is the Co-founder and Head of Quant at Roseon.Finance
- Defying the Traditional Trends by Helping Investors Make Confident Crypto Decisions with Imgesu Cetin
- Exploiting Nudge Economics and Blockchain Technology to Disrupt the $200 Billion Rewards Points Industry

- From Financial Markets to Decentralized Leveraged Markets, with Vaibhav Kadikar, CloseCross
- How to predict rug pulls when making crypto investments and donations Nick Smart
- How to Review and Rate Decentralized Finance (DeFi) Protocols with Rex Hygate at DeFi Safety
- How to set up a crypto Cayman fund and a crypto license in Lithuania
- How to Solve the Oracle Dilemma and Entropy using SupraOracles, with Joshua Tobkin34:061310Published5/7/22
- Mitigating Crypto Control Risks and What Future Banks and DeFi Products Look Like for Investors, with Philipp Pieper and Swarm Markets
- The challenges of driving crypto adoption, Rosario Ingargiola, Bosonic Digital
- The importance of Financial Smart Contracts, Ralf Kubli, Casper Association

TREES, BIRDS, AND FIRE

- The Importance of Technology Investing for Women, Angelika Dehmel, BUX
- The Intersection of Social, Economic and Technology Advancements with a Developer Blockchain Toolkit
- Transfer Agency and Japanese Banking, with Jamie Finn, Co-Founder at Securitize
- Transfer Agency as a "Good Control Location" for Cryptocurrencies, Scott Harrigan
- Transitioning from Traditional Finance to Decentralized Finance : Creating and Building DeFi products and protocols with Bifrost
- Ushering in a prosperous new future with Decentralized Finance, App-chains, and a solution for the centralized finance Trust deficit, with Barney Mannerings @ Vega Protocol
- Helping the Traditional Financial World Evolve to a Decentralized Multi-Chain

Future with d-Wallets and Multi-Chain Bridges, Sean Lee @ ODSY Network

Blockchain Ethics

- A Brave New World: The Power of Building an Altruistic Global Society, with Fran Strajnar
- A Father's Journey to Humanity; and a Criminal Complaint to the U.S. Department of Justice, with James Ryan @ Omgeneum
- Blockchain for Good, Helen Hai, United Nations Goodwill Ambassador for Industrialization in Africa
- Building an Ethical Hedge and Thoughts on Charlie Lee and Elon Musk with Litecoin Foundation Director David Schwartz
- Inspiring Digital futures in Afghanistan for women, Fereshteh Forough Code to Inspire
- Lessons from the Bitfinex Hack and Mars Stealer Malware Threats, Justin Choo, Cabital

- The importance of Blockchain Ethics with David Kay, Liti Capital
- Using Blockchain to Reunite Families, Kristine Smith
- A Father's Journey for Humanity; and a Criminal Complaint to the U.S. Department of Justice, with James Ryan @ Omgeneum

Gaming

- Betting Big on In-Game Fantasy Sports Betting and the Future of Rugby, Paddy Power
- Building Gaming Communities with WAX and Blockchain Brawlers, Michael Rubinelli
- E-sports, Decentralized Gaming, and the Building of a brand new industry: Money Sports, with J.D. Salbego and AnRKey X
- How to build a blockchain gaming platform, Gregory Crous, H3RO3S
- How to navigate global gaming challenges, Don Norbury, Shrapnel

TREES, BIRDS, AND FIRE

- NFT gaming trends to watch with Ishan NegiIshan, Polygon Studios
- The Impact of Covid on the Future of eSports and Live Gaming, with Joseph Chong and the League of Ancients
- Verge Crypto, Quantum, Casino Coins, and Cyber Insights with Mark Wittenberg and Mihael Radoslovic
- Virtual Reality Gaming, Crypto Insights from Miami, Jonathan Ovadia, AEXLab

Leadership

- Betting Your Future with Conviction in BolieCoin, with Craig Curtis
- Bitcoin, ten years on the roller coaster, and where it may go next, insights with crypto legend Charlie Shrem
- Blockchain, Pandemics, and Utility Tokens from the Founder of Fortitude Ranch, Dr. Drew Miller

- Building a Collaborative Decentralized Society through Servant Leadership, Cyrus Taghehchian, CEO, Splyt Core Foundation
- Building a Resilient Skill Set for the Decentralized Economy, with Leigh Cuen
- Creating healthy ecosystems and a sustainable future with Sebnem Rusitschka, Crypto Token Flower
- How algorithmic search applications can help in finance, Meir Shachar, Powerlinx
- How Building a Data-Driven Health-Focused Organization During the Coronavirus Pandemic Won the Admiration and Support of the National Science Foundation and the Blockchain Industry, with Susan Joseph
- How street smarts and thinking on your feet can take you a long, long way: tech & crypto insights with Monty Munford, Sienna Network
- How the PadawanDAO can help students to go to blockchain conferences Eason Wu, TKS

TREES, BIRDS, AND FIRE

- Innovation insights with Samaira Mehta, a 13 year old TIME Young Leader Shaping the Decade
- Rolling with the Punches: How JUSTTIP is transforming the service sector for tipped employees in Ireland
- The Knowledge Society, Creating Global Social and Economic Reform, Navid Nathoo
- The Roles of Existentialism, Nihilism, and Nondualism in Emerging Technologies, Blockchain and Quantum Computing
- Using Blockchain to achieve Global Social Impact, Samantha Ouyang

Metaverses

- Building a Better Metaverse with Better Architecture, with Tomas Zacek
- Building the Infrastructure for Decentralized Identity within the Metaverse, Enjin Rene Stefancic

- Building the metaverse city of Lobsteropolis - the future of lobsters as sentient and metaversal beings.
- Building the Metaverse, insights with Simon Kertonegoro, My Metaverse
- Building the world's premier luxury branded metaverse mall
- Live from Davos, Switzerland, global leader in cryptocurrencies, Felix Honigwachs
- Navigating Your Hyper-Real Synthetic Likeness in the Metaverse with Deep Fakes, Tom Graham
- NFTs and Building the Metaverse with Jamie Goldblatt and Mind Chill 360 Media
- Real Estate Development Opportunities in the Metaverse, Erin Sykes
- Staying Safe in the Metaverse and the Private Key Paradox, Ruben Merre
- Stepping into the Metaverse: Building Digital DisneyLand with Michael Dowling, Finance Professor at Dublin City University

TREES, BIRDS, AND FIRE

- The challenges of building a metaverse entertainment platform, insights with Colin Fitzpatrick, Animal Concerts.
- The value of Industrially Designed 3-Dimensional Metaverse Marketplaces, insights with Julian Picaza, SmartMFG
- Using the Metaverse to Transform Logistics, Sandeep Aggarwal, Logix
- Creating Metaverse Experiences, Leaving a Legacy, and Bringing Tupac Back to Life, with Justin Trevor Winters @ Verified Labs

Mobility

- Achieving Sustainability in Fleet Management with a Unique Electrical Vehicle Data Approach, with Geotab and David Savage
- Building a Scooter-Based Eco-Friendly Transportation Infrastructure as Mobility Done Right, with Charlie Gleeson and Zipp Mobility

Non-Fungible Tokens

- A Brand New World of BioDiversity and Wild Animal Conservation with Wild Earth NFT
- Building a Blueprint for Trust, Thoughts on Spencer Dinwiddie and The Role of Hedera Hashgraph in Blockchain Governance, with Dr. Leemon Baird
- Building an NFT Marketplace for Global Healthcare, Dr. Michael J Kaldasch, Almedis Blockchain
- Building Communities through NFTs, with Matt Street, Lucky Maneki NFT
- Conducting Early Stage Market Validation and Building No-Code Storefronts for NFTs and Web 3.0
- Creating art and smart rings from microbes and biology-based NFTs, David Kvitsiani, CNICK

TREES, BIRDS, AND FIRE

- Crypto from the Red Carpet: Celebrity NFT and Metaverse Insights with Entertainment Producer Sophie Watts
- Empowering Women and creating Fair Labor in the Fashion Supply Chain, Lindsey Mallon
- Gardening and Sculpture NFTs can create a healthy mindset, Ken Folan, Kildare Gallery
- How Abstract Artists can Start to Create NFTs on OpenSea and use them for Philanthropy
- How Cannabis and Crypto are Helping This Artist Survive Terminal Cancer, with Arabella Proffer
- How more women can become involved in NFTs, Sara Nemati, artist and contributor Bored Ape Ladies NFT collective
- How Tapping into Our Creativity and Memories can Eradicate Toxic Happiness and Improve Mental Health

TREES, BIRDS, AND FIRE

- How to Create Limited Edition NFTs with Amelia Tomasicchio at the Cryptonomist
- How to earn Royalties with Lithographic Prints using Zero Knowledge Proofs, with TreeTrunk and John Wolpert
- How to rate Celebrity NFTs, insights with Joey Dunne, aka LeDrop WithCheese
- Incorporating Cutting-Edge Digital Technologies while Building Digital Production Systems, Dilek Sezen, TreeTrunk
- Indexing, Swapping, and Aggregating Non Fungible Tokens, with Ori Levi and NFTrade
- Initial NFT Offerings with Steve Good and Dreams Quest
- Ksoids, Orangutans, and the Opportunity to Impact Our Global Carbon Footprint with NFTs, with Danil Kviroruchko and Andy Alexhin
- NFTs for dummies, art, investments, crypto punks and more all explained with Jamil Hasan & Jillian Godsil

TREES, BIRDS, AND FIRE

- Painting the Invisible - How Artists and Scientists are paving the path for NFTs in film and painting with Christian Hook
- Repurposing AK47s for peace, CRYPTO KALASH stories with Bran Symondson
- Reshaping the Diamond Industry with Consortiums, NFTs, and Blockchained Supply Chains with Diamante Blockchain and Chirag Jetani
- Retro Cat NFTs, Korean inspirations with artist Stephanie Ishler
- SHABANG!!: Discovering your inner NFT with world famous photographer Peter Hurley
- Sold Out in 15 Seconds: How Graffiti Kings and Street Art are Capturing the NFT Art World's Attention and Trust, Darren Cullen aka SER
- Squirrel Syndrome: Why chasing 'Bright and Shiny' in Gaming NFTs often leaves investors and gamers empty handed, Jawad Ashraf

- The Collector's Dilemma, Role of Crypto Experts, and the Intersection of NFTs and Blockchain Innovation with Sarina Charugundla
- The duality of life as half man, half cyborg, crypto and NFT insights with collective conscious artist Orrin
- The NFT Handbook - Obtaining a Comprehensive Overview of the Global NFT Market with QuHarrison Terry
- The Role of Enthusiasm and the Importance of Winning in Crypto With Tally Founder, Dennison Bertram
- What NFT Life is Like as an Original CryptoPunk
- Why NFT Birds are better than Punks, Apes and Horses, with Daniel Steeves and tudaBirds
- Building a Nifty, Resurgent Web 3.0 Movement for NFT Content Creators, with the Nexus Voyagers' Network, with Ben and Miles

TREES, BIRDS, AND FIRE

- Making NFT & Cryptocurrency Part of Mainstream Everyday Life, with Julian Rodriguez @ Momento NFT
- How ConsenSys Mesh Helps Blockchain Founders Build for the Future, Even During the Harshest Market Conditions, with Shawn Cheng

Public Relations / Marketing

- A better future for online content and streaming in a post Youtube world with Jeremy Kauffman, Founder LBRY, Odysee
- B2B and Healthcare Insights and the Role of Influence in Social Media, with Evan Kirstel
- How to do PR right in the Crypto world, Armel Leslie, Peaks Strategies
- Mining Website Traffic and Social Media to Build Publishers' Internet Presence, Reggie Jerath, Gather

- What to Look Forward to the Most During Istanbul Blockchain Week, with Erhan Korhaliller
- Why crypto adoption is coming sooner than you think, Michael Casey, CoinDesk

Regulatory Frameworks

- Alleviating Data Protection Risks with Multi-Party Computation and Partisia Blockchain, Kurt Neilsen
- Challenges and Opportunities with Developing a Global Crypto Regulatory Framework, William Je
- Creating a Regulatory Framework for the Collaborative Decentralized World, with Li Jun, Founder of Ontology
- Decentralized Finance Yield, Regulatory Compliance, and Building Compliant Platforms, Raymond Hsu, Cabital.

- Security Tokens, Energy Tokenization and Regulatory Lessons from the Middle East, with Walid Abou Zaki
- Setting codes of conduct and best AML/KYC practices for the virtual assets, Malcolm Wright, Global Digital Finance

Space

- Not So Lost in Space: Living Forever, Creating Environmental Sustainability, and Crowd-Funding Lessons from the Space Economy, with Samson Williams
- Space as a Service, Lessons from Space, with Zee Zheng and SpaceChain

Trading and Investing

- Building the next generation alternative investment banking, Paulius Stankevicius

TREES, BIRDS, AND FIRE

- How to Overcome Depression When Trading and Investing in Cryptocurrencies, with Jay H. Tepley
- Institutional Insights: Bitcoin, Ethereum, Tether, and Altcoin Market Analysis with Mike McGlone
- Pitfalls and Rewards of Options Trading with 100X Leverage and its Impact on India's Crypto Adoption
- Starting from Zero and Challenges with Deep Tech Investing, with Sonny Vu and AREVO
- Tech, security and global crypto growth insights with Samy Karim Binance Smart Chain Ecosystem
- The Shadow CEO, and former poker pro, Athan Slotkin, shares his crypto investing tips for professional and college students new to the cryptosphere.
- VC Investing in Projects with Usability and Sustainability, Rui Zhang, gumi Cryptos Capital

Web 3.0

- Building the Web 3.0 with Deeper Network's decentralized VPNs, with Eric Ma
- Controlling and Sharing your Data with Data Unions, Ethereum maximalist Shiv Malik
- Effectively Transitioning Clients to the Web 3.0 Economy by Doing Public Relations Right and Building the Crypto PR Firm of the Future, with Kurt Ivy @ Simple Crypto PR
- The Race Against an Orwellian Future is ON, Let's Go!!, with Geoff McCabe @ LetsGo
- What you need to know about Web 3.0 with Jeremy Lindblad and Chibi Dinos
- Why Artists Should Create Their Own Platforms for Fan Engagement, DJ Sam Feldt, Fangage
- Winning the Churn Wars and Creating Lifetime Value through Digital Streaming in the Web 3.0 Economy, with Andrea Berry @ Theta Labs

TREES, BIRDS, AND FIRE

- What's in the Store Now That the Mass Exodus from Web 2 to Web 3.0 Has Begun? With Eric McHugh @ SHOPX
- Behind the Creation of a Tokenized Utility Platform that helps Those With Autism, Mental Health, and Special Needs Achieve Disability Rights, Barry Mezey @ KWAN 2.0

TREES, BIRDS, AND FIRE

Appendix C: Crypto Hipster's Chronicles

These are a combination of three to five clips from the Crypto Hipster Podcasts by common theme, thread of topic. A complete list of Jamil's Crypto Hipster's Chronicles is presented below. All of them can be found at anchor.fm/crypto-hipster-podcast and can be listened to on Spotify, Apple Podcasts, Amazon, Anchor, or wherever enjoy your favorite podcasts.

- Episode 1: Unstoppable Authors
- Episode 2: DeFi: Why Wall Street is Running Scared
- Episode 3: Metaverse Metamorphosis
- Episode 4: The Pursuit of Trust and Altruistic Good

TREES, BIRDS, AND FIRE

- Episode 5: Crypto Gaming Ancients and Heroes
- Episode 6: Lobsters, Apes, Stars and Orangutans
- Episode 7: Hacks, Rugs, and the Court Jester
- Episode 8: NFTs Arising from the Ashes
- Episode 9: Knowledge is Power
- Episode 10: Leveraging Web 3.0 to Build Fan Engagement
- Episode 11: Overcoming Adversity and Building Resiliency through NFTs
- Episode 12: Ukraine: A State in a Smartphone
- Episode 13: Travelling Through Space and Time
- Episode 14: Research, Development, and Production in Crypto-Gaming and the Metaverse
- Episode 15: Early Web 3 and NFT Marketplaces

TREES, BIRDS, AND FIRE

- Episode 16: Going Above and Beyond to Create a World of Heroes
- Episode 17: Addressing Compliance and Global Regulatory Standards
- Episode 18: Achieving Global Sustainability Goals through Bitcoin Mining and Community Coins
- Episode 19: Early Crypto Trends and Predictions for 2022
- Episode 20: Controlling and Securing Your Personal Web 3 Data and Online Identity
- Episode 21: Breaking: Wall Street!! Why?: Bitcoin
- Episode 22: Crypto Valley Insights: How Switzerland is Poised to Become the Global Crypto Leader
- Episode 23: The Three Musketeers of DAOs (Decentralized Autonomous Organizations) – Governance, Intelligence, and Justice
- Episode 24: How Crypto is Solving the Carbon Neutrality Crisis

TREES, BIRDS, AND FIRE

- Episode 25: Bitcoin: Are We Achieving Satoshi's Vision?
- Episode 26: Crypto 101: Building a Resiliency Skillset
- Episode 27: War Games, Altruism, and Blockchain for Peace
- Episode 28: DEFI-ing the Future of Finance for Retail and Institutional Crypto Adoption
- Episode 29: Uplifting Creators and Collectors through Cutting-Edge Technologies and Innovation (featuring Tree Trunk)
- Episode 30: Ethics, Conviction, and Resiliency – Important Personal Traits or Blockchain Cornerstones?
- Episode 31: Funds, Crypto Banks, and Direct Investments – Doing DeFi in Different Ways
- Episode 32: Building Equitable Futures and Healthy Ecosystems with Crypto Tokens, NFTs, and Metaverses

- Episode 33: Discovering Your Inner NFT in the Real World and the Metaverse
- Episode 34: Crypto Hipster Podcast's Submission to Irish Podcast Awards for Podcast of the Year
- Episode 35: A Critical Look For Us Beyond Just Web 3.0
- Episode 36: Starting from Zero: How to Build a Powerful Personal Blueprint for Success
- Episode 37: Helping Online Publishers Build Bright and Abundant Futures
- Episode 38: The Pitfalls and Rewards of Crypto Trading and Investing
- Episode 39: Malware, Gem Wear, and Underwear: Measuring Blockchain's Beneficial Impact on Disparate Industries
- Episode 40: Land Grab! Empowering Real Estate Owners and Healthcare Participants in the Web 3.0 Economy

TREES, BIRDS, AND FIRE

- Episode 41: Crypto Across the 4 Corners: Blockchain and Bitcoin Insights from Around the World
- Episode 42: Creating a Path Forward in Decentralized Finance for Global Banks and Institutions
- Episode 43: The Strength of the Triangle Mindset: Leveraging the Intersection of Artificial Intelligence, Machine Learning and Blockchain Technology to Benefit Humanity
- Episode 44: Why Economists and Environmentalists Are Often WRONG About Bitcoin
- Episode 45: The Digital Crypto Future is Coming Sooner Than You Think

www.ingramcontent.com/pod-product-compliance
Lightning Source LLC
Chambersburg PA
CBHW071409210526
45465CB00001B/315